PRINT AND CURSIVE
HANDWRITING WORKBOOK

Print and Cursive Handwriting Workbook

35 Lessons to Improve Your Penmanship

SALLY SANDERS

ROCKRIDGE
PRESS

For general information on our other products and services or to obtain technical support, please contact our Customer Care Department within the United States at (866) 744-2665, or outside the United States at (510) 253-0500.

Rockridge Press publishes its books in a variety of electronic and print formats. Some content that appears in print may not be available in electronic books, and vice versa.

Interior and Cover Designer: Jami Spittler
Art Producer: Sue Smith
Editor: Justin Hartung
Production Manager: Oriana Siska
Production Editor: Melissa Edeburn

Photography and Illustration © Sally Sanders

ISBN: Print 978-1-64152-417-9

R0

for my children & grandchildren

Contents

Introduction

No two people have the same handwriting. Your handwriting is your unique stamp, used to prove your identity when you sign a legal document. But it can also provide a personal touch on birthday cards, love letters, or professional thank-you notes. It's too bad, then, that so many people are embarrassed by their handwriting, believing it to be illegible, childish, or otherwise failing to represent them as they wish to be perceived. Even people with good handwriting run the risk of falling into lazy habits. Fortunately, with a little practice you can improve your handwriting so that it's something you can display with pride.

Writing by hand can be therapeutic and meditative, engaging your brain in ways that typing does not. Studies have demonstrated that taking notes by hand improves your subject matter retention. A journal can be a space to clarify your thoughts, get emotions out of your head, solve problems and . . . practice your handwriting!

I have long admired elegant penmanship, and in grade school I received praise for my beautiful, loopy, flowing hand. Unfortunately, when I had to speed up my writing for note-taking, it fell apart. It turns out the loopy hand many of us learned in grade school is a terrible model for the fast handwriting our lives require.

Because the lovely, flourished handwriting we learned in grade school is bound to diminish when we write quickly, it's really not our fault if our writing now looks

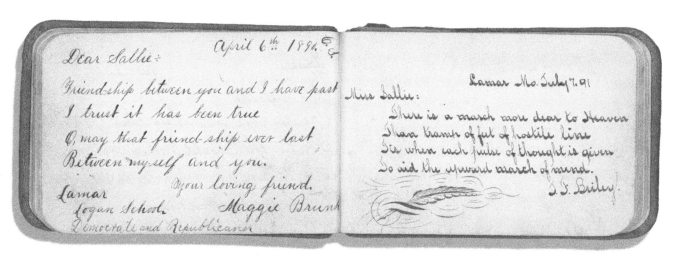

Beautiful handwriting examples as taught in school in the late 1800s. This style was definitely not designed for speed.

sloppy, messy, or careless. We need to relearn proper handwriting, rather than be judged on how inadequate our grade school penmanship model is for real life.

As a professional calligrapher, I have been able to incorporate rules of good design and letterforms into my handwriting, freeing myself from my old illegible scrawl. (But to be clear, handwriting and calligraphy are two very distinct skills.) Through teaching calligraphy to hundreds of students, I've learned how people write, how they learn to write, and how to help them achieve their best handwriting results.

I remember teaching a high school workshop on Gothic calligraphy. My students included gang members. I started them out carefully drawing rows of straight lines, over and over. What followed was a silent classroom of students conscientiously and calmly repeating strokes with perfect pen angles, making beautiful pages. I was surprised and gratified to see that something I find engaging and quieting had the same effect on others, regardless of background.

You may want to improve your handwriting to increase its legibility, to be able to write more quickly, or to write in a way that gives a good first impression. Whatever your reasons, this workbook can help you achieve better penmanship. You'll learn to analyze your handwriting, decipher its weaknesses, and pinpoint the root causes of those weaknesses. This book offers methods and lessons to correct handwriting flaws, and it also provides exercises to help you develop a distinctively unique style.

one

Rediscover the Art of Handwriting

In the Middle Ages, only the elite knew how to write—and they liked to keep it that way. Written communication and all its benefits were restricted to members of the church and ruling class. In our modern society, writing is a basic requirement of every child. But because we now use keyboards as our primary tool for writing, many people don't develop or maintain their handwriting skills. In this chapter, you'll learn about the benefits of good handwriting and how to improve your own.

The Importance of Handwriting

In a society accustomed to communicating by typing, why do we need to have good handwriting? One reason is that when handwriting *is* required, there's no shortcut to improve it right before you need to use it. Have you ever felt like you could have provided a more professional note to your colleague, or drafted a more attractive and legible sympathy card? Good handwriting is a little like a quiz for which you neglected to study.

There are many benefits to be gained in your professional and personal life by taking the time to learn clear, attractive handwriting.

A 2014 *Psychological Science* research article describes studies showing that writing by hand rather than typing improves retention. Even though typing can produce heard speech nearly verbatim, handwritten notes allow writers to internalize and analyze oral information as they write. When two groups (one hand writing notes during a lecture, the other typing them) are tested, the longhand group remembers more from the lecture than the typing group. In the long run, schools that skimp on teaching handwriting might be doing students a disservice.

Writing legibly is crucial in some professions. Misinterpretation of prescriptions was estimated by the Agency for Healthcare Research and Quality in 2010 to result in a direct cost of hundreds of millions of dollars each year for the Medicare population alone. That cost is due to adverse drug effects.

Poor handwriting can hurt you professionally. Illegible handwritten notes and edits to hard copy drafts can waste the time of colleagues who have to decipher them—costly to the business and embarrassing for the note writer. And if your job requires regular note-taking, you may be especially concerned about speed and legibility when passing on the information you transcribe.

Business experts preach about the necessity of personal communication with clients and customers, and they often advise the sending of handwritten notes to express thanks or encouragement.

If you're a student, the benefits of handwriting extend beyond the aforementioned improved retention that comes from handwritten note-taking. Many exams still need to be taken by hand, and your writing should not bog you down. It should be efficient, leaving you free to put your best foot forward, academically.

There's also the matter of privacy, which we all know isn't much of a guarantee when sending a message by digital communication. Handwritten messages avoid that risk, and there's also much less chance of writing the wrong address on a handwritten envelope than of sending an email or text to an unintended recipient.

By Hand Is by Heart

Handwritten letters are mentioned in *The Iliad*, which was written ten thousand years ago, and there's no reason to think handwritten letters won't continue to be an important way of communicating for years to come. By handwriting a card or letter, you're honoring the recipient with your time and energy. Adding a handwritten note or letter to a card personalizes it and adds depth to your greeting. Moreover, your handwriting offers the recipient a glimpse of who you are.

It is a welcome surprise to pick up your mail and see a hand-addressed envelope. You often recognize the writing or unconsciously respond to the character embedded in the writing. You open the letter first, or you lay it aside to be savored after the business mail has been addressed.

Here are some ways in which handwriting can enrich your personal communications:

▶ Handwritten letters sent to friends and family hold special value because they can hold the memory of your loved ones spelling out their love and concern and passing along their wisdom.

▶ Handwritten lunchbox notes are a fun way to let children know they are loved, and such notes can brighten up their day with an inside joke, a riddle, silly song, or special greeting.

▶ Sympathy notes are especially important to write by hand. They show that you are concerned enough to give them something to hold as they read your heartwarming words.

▶ Handwritten postcards are a fun way to let your loved ones know about your adventures. They get a visual as well as written message, and you have the pleasure of selecting the cards.

▶ Finally, a thank-you note says so much more when the receiver sees that you have taken the time to write it by hand. It can evoke the memory of time spent together or heighten expressions of gratitude for a special gift.

Old postcards from a secondhand bookseller on the bank of the River Seine

Five Common Handwriting Problems

What is it about your handwriting that urged you to pick up this book? Is it speed you want? More legibility? More personality? Before you can improve your handwriting, you need to determine what is causing it to look bad. Good handwriting is legible, flowing, consistent, and personal. We will look here at different ways your writing can fall short, so you can determine which of the workbook activities will help you correct it. Be ruthless when looking at your writing. The more you can pinpoint your imperfections, the better you will be at fixing them. Make a list of the concerns you have when you look at your writing and determine your priorities. With your list and goals in hand, you can start working on the exercises. Start slowly and follow the exercises with an open mind. You are teaching your hand, eye, and brain to do new things, or at least things they haven't focused on in many years.

Keep in mind that most people maintain three styles of handwriting: one for writing only they will read, one for writing that will be shared with other people, and one, their best, for formal communications and cards. This book focuses mainly on handwriting for shared, nonformal communications, though chapter 5 covers handwriting for formal communications.

Most of us have handwriting problems that started in grade school, about the time we needed to start writing more and writing faster. One friend related that in the 6th grade his teachers would ask, "How can you be so smart and still have such bad handwriting?" This feedback spurred him to develop a style of handwriting that is fast but highly legible. He is happy with the way it reflects on him as a person, and he is pleased when colleagues invite him to write messages on office cards.

Find a paragraph or two that you've written in your everyday style, or write down something right now. If you can't think of anything, just write down the words of a song or something you know by heart. Then take a good look: Which common handwriting issues are you demonstrating? Get out your red pen and mark them up! (And don't worry, we'll have tackled them all by the end of this book.)

LOVE Sculpture
Perhaps the most familiar of Philadelphia's many artworks

LOVE sculpture
Perhaps the most familiar of Philidelphia's many artworks

Perhaps

1. WHAT'S THAT LETTER?

Poor letter formation can stem from using elaborate, heavily flourished models for quick writing. With speed, your loops and details might overwhelm the shapes of the letters. Maybe you leave your a's open at the top and they look like u's. Maybe your i's look like e's. A lot of people leave out the first stroke of m and n. Maybe you start a letter at an awkward point, so the joins don't work or the letters have a weird shape. Or maybe you aren't sure just how to form a particular letter. All these problems are fixable.

The italic alphabet in chapter 3 (lessons 9 to 12, see pages 35 to 44) is made for speed and will show you the best way to form your letters and group them according to related shapes. Your finished writing may end up looking nothing like italic, but its underlying rules will help you clarify your letterforms within your own style.

You may appreciate the "ball-and-stick" printing in chapter 3 (lessons 6 and 7, see pages 28 to 32), especially if you prefer block lettering or "printing" to cursive handwriting and want to clarify your letterforms. You will also find help dealing with letter joins in chapter 4 (lessons 14 to 19, see pages 46 to 68). Sometimes the join can loop into a letterform or change shape or direction, thereby making words illegible. Think the tops of your letters don't matter all that much? Just place a card or ruler horizontally over a line of type. Notice that the sentence is readable with just a little of the letters' *skyline* (the top third of the letter height) visible. So be careful as you round the top of the second stroke of n's or make the sharp turnaround at the *waistline* (an imaginary guideline for the height of lowercase letters) in your u's. These strokes all make a difference to the legibility of your writing.

These letterforms have strayed so far from their original form that they are almost illegible. This writer could review/learn the italic alphabet in lessons 9 to 12 (see pages 35 to 44) and also review letter joins in chapter 4 (lessons 14 to 19, see pages 46 to 68) to gain control and legibility.

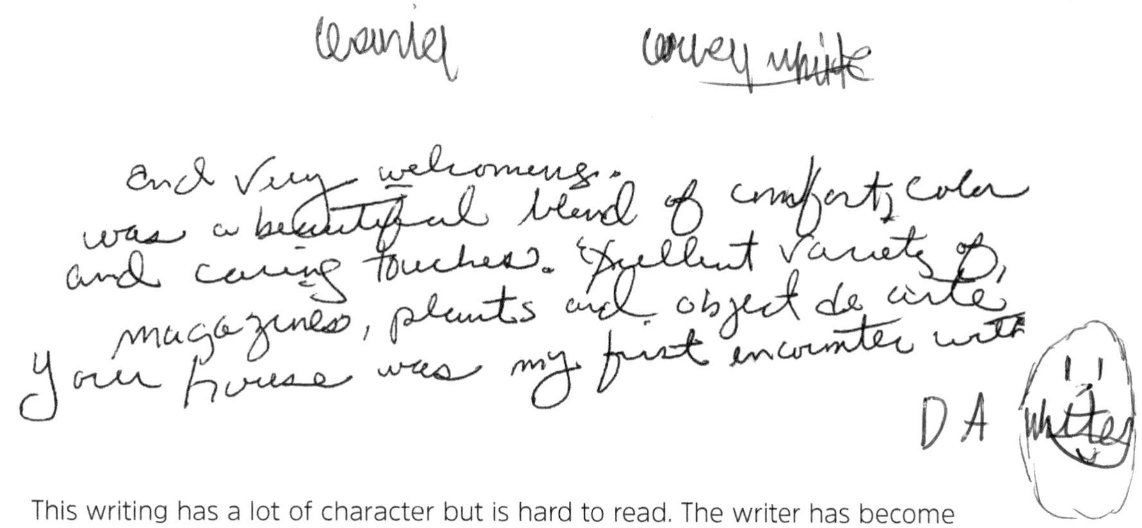

[handwritten sample]

This writing has a lot of character but is hard to read. The writer has become rather lax about letterforms. For example, the a's, n's, and u's all look alike. The r's don't have enough shape for readers to distinguish them from i's. The letters' *slope* (lean) is inconsistent, inhibiting any natural flow. The joined g's are formed with a unique *ductus* (stroke sequence) which can be kept because it is readable and adds personality. The writer could improve letter formation and joins by reviewing lessons 9 to 12 and 14 to 19 (see pages 35 to 44 and 46 to 68), and practice controlling the slope with lesson 5 (see page 24).

2. JUST PLAIN WACKY

Consistency is a must. Good handwriting has even rhythm, size, slope, and spacing. Tension in your body will translate directly into your writing, inhibiting your natural flow and perhaps leading to inconsistent letterforms. You may use several types of b's, for example, or slant your letters in all different directions. Whether your slope is forward or backward (or you have no slope at all) isn't your biggest problem; rather, it is too much variation.

Simplification is an important design concept, and one that will serve you well as you train your hand to write more evenly. Start with the exercises in chapter 2 (lesson 5, see page 24) and return to them often to train your muscles. Through repetition of these exercises, you will begin to discover your own natural slope and rhythm.

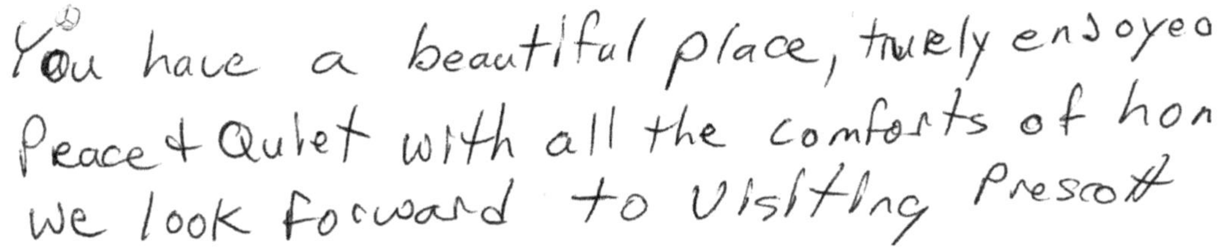

[handwritten sample]

This writing doesn't join up at all and is inconsistent in letter size and slope. The letters lean in all different directions. This inconsistency might be because of tension or because the pen is pressed a little too firmly on the paper (you can see the tension by looking at the dots over the i's). Checking pen hold, repeating the slope exercises in lesson 5 (see page 24), and revisiting letter formation in lessons 6 and 7 (see pages 28 to 32) will be helpful.

3. SPEED CONTROL

Speed can be a reason for poor handwriting. Compared with cursive alphabets, printed alphabets take a little longer to write because of all the pen lifts. Nevertheless, when written at a comfortable pace, printing can have as even a rhythm as cursive handwriting.

Cursive is often written too quickly for legibility. To speed up your writing without losing legibility, eliminate loops from letters. Not every letter needs to be joined up.

Thinking faster than we can write leads to writing too fast. If this is your downfall, try changing how much you write. When you are taking notes or jotting down thoughts, try capturing the important ideas in unfinished sentences, and go back when you have a chance to fill out the thought with more words. Some people find it effective to leave out the verbs and add them later. Or you might write concepts in a list or outline form, leaving room to fill them in later.

This handwriting sample reflects faster thinking than writing. Letters are omitted, and almost every curve has become a sharp zigzag. Going just a bit more slowly (if possible) would help with legibility. Practice with joins (chapter 4, lessons 14 to 19, see pages 46 to 68) and letterforms will help later when speed is required.

Yesterday the sun was out so I went Running, I come to the llama field and called them over, there was a dense fog there, with tall pines on the other side of the field behind the llamas and the sun rising behind all that sending Big Bible rays up and all around the llamas, the scene made me forget where I was!

This sample also reflects quick writing, as evidenced by the opening up of some of the a's and extra loops on some letters. But the writer has struck a good balance between speed and legibility. A vigorous and consistent slope helps hold everything together. The stronger your handwriting, the more it can survive the strain of speed.

4. DOES SIZE MATTER?

A little. Both small and large handwriting are acceptable, but a small script is harder to read than a large script, and oversized writing can look childish or pompous. (Just who was John Hancock anyway?) You should aim for a middle ground.

A quick fix for tiny writing is to increase the size of your pen tip (try a medium-tip pen if you normally use a fine-tip point). This change encourages you to enlarge your letterforms. Switch back to your favorite pen tip size while keeping your new larger writing.

To fix overly large script, use guidelines while you retrain your fingers. Concentrate on keeping letter width consistent and proportionate to letter height. The italic alphabet in chapter 3 illustrates standard letter-width proportions.

Your beautiful presentation piece for Ted Turner was a highlight of our joint meeting of the Two Circles.

Beautiful handwriting but a little small for most occasions.

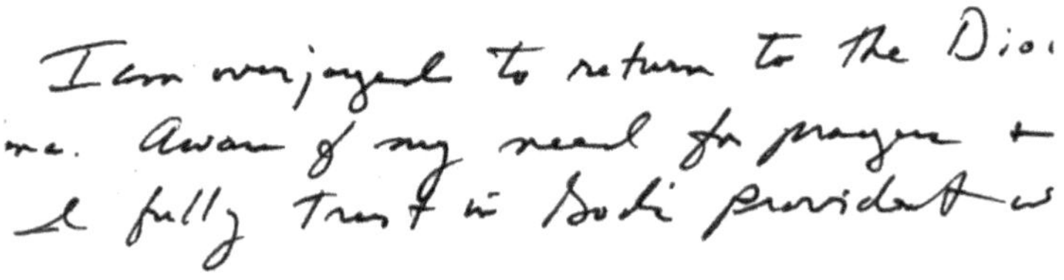

This handwriting is a bit small and hard to read.

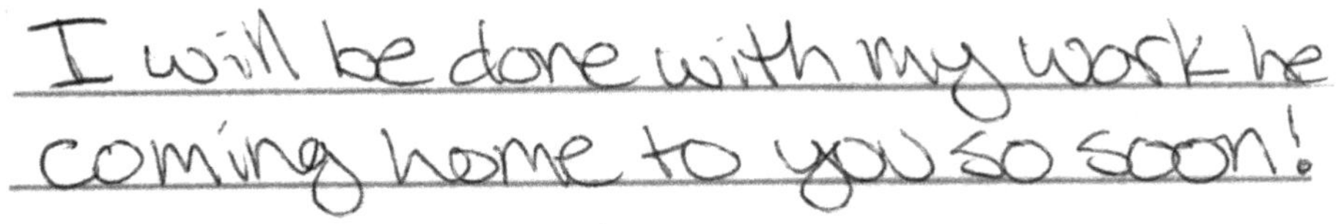
I will be done with my work be
coming home to you so soon!

This handwriting is a little large and suggests a young writer.

5. BABY FACE

A surprising quality of immature-looking handwriting is a hand that is "too nice" and adheres too closely to the school model. Perfectly copied letters need some inconsistencies and personalization to truly belong to an adult writer. Writing too large or too loopy can look juvenile or fussy. Unjoined letters can also look childish. Writers with these issues will benefit from learning the italic letterforms in chapter 3 (lessons 9 to 12, see pages 35 to 44) and practicing joining (chapter 4, see page 49). The techniques in chapter 5 (lessons 26 and 27, see pages 98 to 105) will help writers personalize their handwriting.

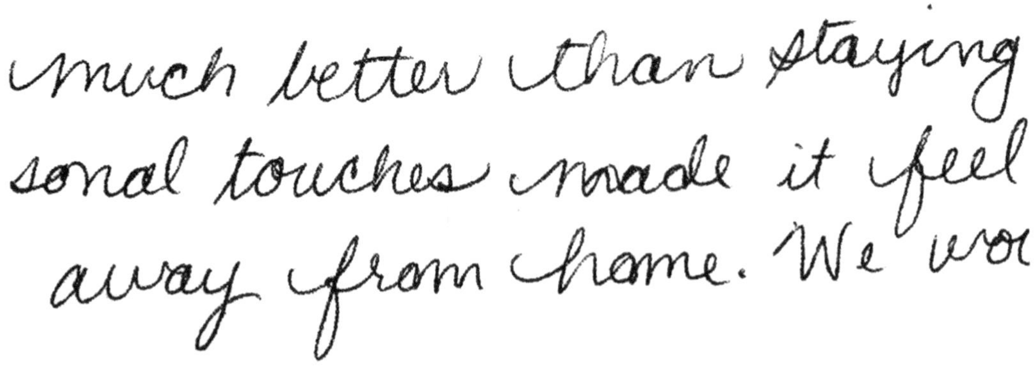
much better than staying
sonal touches made it feel
away from home. We wo

This writing is a little too close to the model learned in school. Practicing the exercises in chapter 5 (see page 97) to individualize the writing would add a bit of style.

college drop off ♡
We will be back many tin
as our daughter loues her
school & this lovely town.

The larger size of this writing, the lack of a slope, and the overall roundness of the strokes give this writing a somewhat childish look. Chapter 5 (lessons 26 and 27, see pages 98 to 105) will be helpful.

Practice Makes Perfect

Muscle memory, known in neuroscience as motor memory, is a powerful thing. Muscle memory keeps bike riding skills fresh in our minds, it allows us to button a shirt or tie a shoe without thinking about what we're doing, and it is what we need to retrain so that we fix our handwriting. Of course, our muscles don't actually remember anything; our brains do. Motor skills are learned and remembered with repetition. Repetition fires up synapses in the brain, leading to a memory that makes an action or sequence of actions automatic. We depend on muscle memory in handwriting to concentrate on *what* we are writing rather than *how* our hand is forming the letters.

The only problem with muscle memory is that it will retain wobbly letters as well as perfect ones, depending on which are most practiced. Therefore, we need to do the exercises slowly and carefully, making sure that our letters are drawn correctly. A page of wacky strokes is not what we want our hand to "remember." We don't want to reinforce our existing bad handwriting habits. We want to retrain our muscles to make studied movements and thus legible letters.

How to Use This Book

There's a lot packed into this book, which covers 30 lessons in 5 chapters (and includes a bonus chapter with five lessons on calligraphy). Some exercises will require more time than others. And don't worry, lefties. There is plenty of advice and help for you, too!

This chapter has analyzed a variety of handwriting issues to help you identify your weaknesses and their causes. Chapters 2, 3, and 4 present methods and lessons to correct weaknesses. Chapter 3 provides an italic handwriting alphabet for those needing help with letter formation. Use this alphabet as a guide to the most efficient way to draw letters. Chapter 4 deals mainly with joining your letters, and chapter 5 is all about making your writing distinctive and your own. Chapter 6 is for those who desire a brief introduction to calligraphy, specifically writing with a broad-edge pen.

In addition to completing this workbook, one of the best things you can do for your handwriting is to start a journal. Purchase a blank, gridded, or lined journal that you can carry around and write in every day. Fill the pages with the non-letter exercises as well as your own writing. You can randomly paste in photos or inspiring quotes to write around.

Once you find your perfect pen (lesson 2, see page 18), buy several and keep them with paper wherever you pause during the day. You can do the handwriting exercises anywhere, from the kitchen counter to the easy chair in front of the TV to your bed before going to sleep.

No matter your handwriting weakness and goals, start with the first lesson and work your way through the rest one by one. You will be able to tell whether a lesson pertains directly to your goal, and you can spend as little or as much time as needed on it.

You have decided to improve your writing. You can do it, and you can have a good time as you learn. Repetition is the key to improvement, and you'll eventually find practice soothing and even meditative.

By the time you have reached the end of this book, you will have developed your writing into something you can be proud of. It will more closely reflect who you are, and it will come more easily to you. You will be able to write quickly, clearly, and gracefully, in a style that's your very own. You may even be inspired to master the calligraphy lessons in the final chapter. By meeting your own goals with diligent practice, you will have developed a new extension of your personality, found a new way to present yourself to the world, and mastered a new tool for retaining information and communicating with society: *your* handwriting.

two

Handwriting Basics

Now that you've begun to identify some of the common problems in handwriting and thought about what you'd like to improve, it's time to start your handwriting lessons. This chapter will help you set yourself up for success by showing you how to create the optimal writing environment, find the right pencil or pen, hold your writing utensil, position your paper correctly, and practice warm-ups and strokes to loosen up your hand. Distraction or hand cramping will show in your writing.

As you work your way through the lessons in this book, you'll want to become familiar with these terms:

▶ Ascenders—the parts of certain lowercase letters, such as b and h, that extend above the waistline

▶ Baseline—the bottom of the line on which you're writing

▶ Exit stroke—a diagonal or horizontal stroke leaving one letter and connecting to the next letter

▶ Waistline—an imaginary guideline for the height of lowercase letters; in this book's practice space, the waistline is denoted by the dotted line

Make sure your workspace is well lit and uncluttered. Adjust the light or your position if you find you are writing in your own shadow. You may discover your regular chair is a bit low in relation to your desk or table. You can try adjusting your height by placing a pillow on the chair, or perhaps sit on a stool. You want to sit high enough that your writing arm rests lightly on the table surface. This position will allow your arm to move freely as you write. Sitting up straight will add energy and life to your letters.

Paper placement makes a big difference. Position your paper with the top *right* corner tilted up for right-handers, the top *left* corner tilted up for left-handers. Righties, keep the area you are writing on directly under your line of vision by moving your paper slightly to the left as you write. This technique will keep the slant of your letters the same throughout. Lefties, you will be more comfortable if you keep your paper a bit to the left, in front of your left shoulder as you write.

Regardless of whether you are right- or left-handed, you should move the paper up with your non-writing hand as you write lower and lower lines on the page. Moving the paper up will avoid you crunching your letterforms as a result of crowding your hand close to your body.

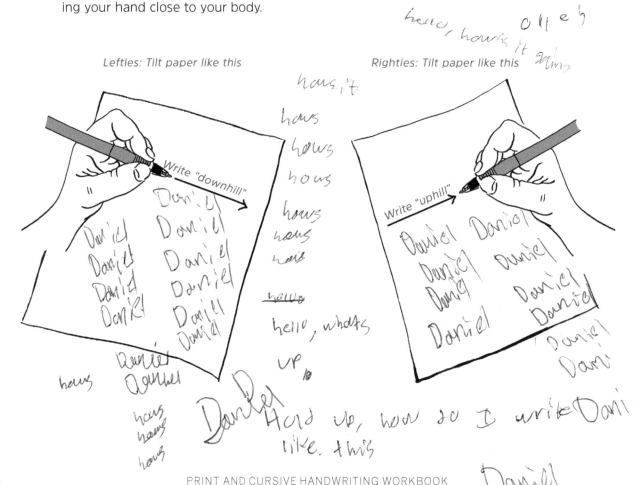

Lefties: Tilt paper like this

Righties: Tilt paper like this

Write "downhill"

Write "uphill"

PRINT AND CURSIVE HANDWRITING WORKBOOK

Are you a lefty who writes with a "hooked" hand, your wrist bent and your hand creeping along above your letters? This technique can be physically fatiguing for your hand, arm, and shoulder, and by extension, your writing may be cramped and awkward. There are several reasons for this awkward way of "over-the-top" writing.

First, the Roman alphabet is written left to right, and lefties find writing from right to left much easier. In fact, the Italian Renaissance genius—and lefty—Leonardo da Vinci wrote his journals from right to left, with all the letters written backward. This trend toward mirror writing (so called because you need to use a mirror to read it) can be seen in some left-handed children who are just beginning to write.

Second, you can thank your early handwriting instructor for your "over-the-top" writing. When you were taught how to write, you were probably made to tilt your paper the same way righties tilt it, rather than the way a lefty needs. With the wrong-tilt, and holding your pen the way righties do, your writing hand blocks your view of the letters, you unavoidably smudge or smear your writing as you move your hand across the page, and your letters slant the wrong way. You therefore learned to place your hand above your writing to avoid these problems.

If this is not a problem for you, there is no need to change your approach. Some lefties are comfortable writing "over-the-top" and need not adjust their hold to improve their handwriting.

If you think you would benefit from a fresh start, simply tilting the left top corner of your paper up and away from you will alleviate the need for the hooked hand. You may find this will ease your writing hand and allow for more graceful movement in your letters. It can take a few weeks of daily practice to retrain your hand to a different hold, but the payoff in speed and comfort of writing can be worth it. If you want to give it a try, place your paper at the new tilt and set it a little to the left of your midline. Adjust the paper to fit you, with your arm, hand, pen, and paper aligned in a comfortable position. Some lefties like to tilt the paper even farther so it is nearly horizontal, making the writing lines close to vertical.

A slanted surface can also help lefties see their writing more easily. Lightly tape your paper onto a drawing board or piece of hardboard, and lift up the edge farthest from you with a few books. Experiment with how high to raise it until you find what suits you best. A good size board for this is 16 to 18 inches by 20 to 24 inches. This size gives you room for your paper and your writing hand. Find a board at an art store, Amazon, or your local lumber store.

TIP: *If your hand is a little shaky, set your non-writing hand on the paper next to your writing hand. Lightly place the index finger of your non-writing hand on your writing hand near the base of your thumb as you write. Surprisingly, this little bit of support can help. A slanted writing surface can also be helpful if you have a tremor.*

The best handwriting paper is smooth but not slick. For pencil writing, it can have a soft "tooth," or slight texture you feel when you lightly rub the paper between your thumb and index finger. When choosing ink, you need to be careful that the paper will not allow the ink to bleed (get fuzzy). The paper can be lined or unlined, but because cursive is often written quickly, lines will help you stay on a horizontal path without slowing you down. Notebooks are great for carrying with you to add minutes of writing practice to your day. Find notebooks in a size convenient for you.

Many people enjoy writing with pencil but find the pencils get dull very fast, making their letterforms thick and blurry. Mechanical pencils can help with this. Try both 7 mm and 5 mm leads to see which you prefer. For the sake of sanity, invest in pencils of higher quality than the multipack disposables that squeak on the paper as you write. Lefties, anything too hard and sharp can cause you problems by digging into the page.

Finding the right pen is a personal quest. At a large stationery store, try out a ballpoint, gel, felt tip, and fountain pen. Do you want a pen that is easily replaceable, or something high quality and classy? Look for a pen with a smooth, even flow; quick-drying ink; and that is a good fit for your hand. Find a tip size that suits your writing mood—fine, medium, or bold. Some pens need to be held more upright than others. Use some of the warm-up strokes in lesson 4 (see page 22) when trying out different pens, or write the same simple phrase with each pen. Eventually you will land on the perfect pen for you.

> **TIP:** If you're a lefty, get a top-bound notebook so the vertical binding doesn't get in your way.

Lefties, you in particular need a smooth, even-flowing ink because you do more pushing than pulling of the pen tip along the paper. A quick-drying ink to prevent smudging is a must. Note that the finer the pen tip, the less ink goes on the page, and the quicker it will dry. The Pilot G2® is readily available, writes smoothly, and dries quickly. If you're having a hard time finding a quick-drying ink, you may be interested in dry gel pens—try the one made by Zebra Sarasa®.

If you'd rather order online, try JetPens.com.

Lefty tripod hold

*Lefty tripod hold with an
ergonomic training grip*

Lefty alternate hold

Use the practice space to see which hold works best for you.

hi

hello, I'm Daniel

Lesson 4 Scribble it out

Before writing, and definitely before beginning each lesson in this workbook, it is important to relax, warm up your muscles, and get the blood flowing. Large arm circles are energizing, and some wild "air writing" (like playing air guitar) is great for getting your mind and body ready to write. Stretch, take some deep breaths, and sit up straight and tall. Be patient with yourself. Worrying about mistakes is not going to help you improve, so just relax into your handwriting session, let your natural rhythm start to develop, and enjoy the time you have set aside for this exercise. With time and diligence, your letterforms will improve, your writing will become more fluid, and your own style will begin to emerge. Here are some good warm-up strokes:

TIP: *If your hand tires during these warm-up strokes, check your posture, paper placement, and try adjusting your pen hold.*

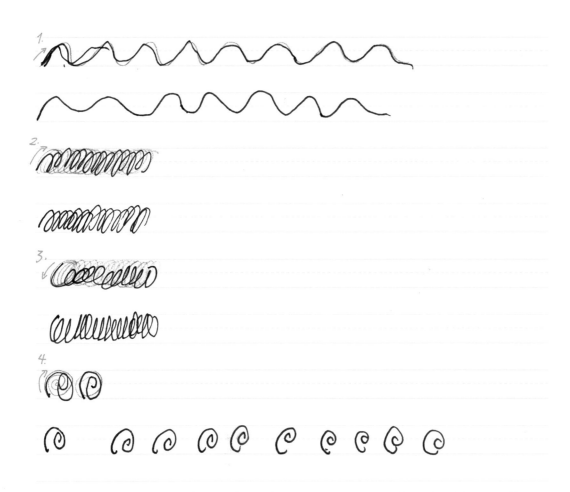

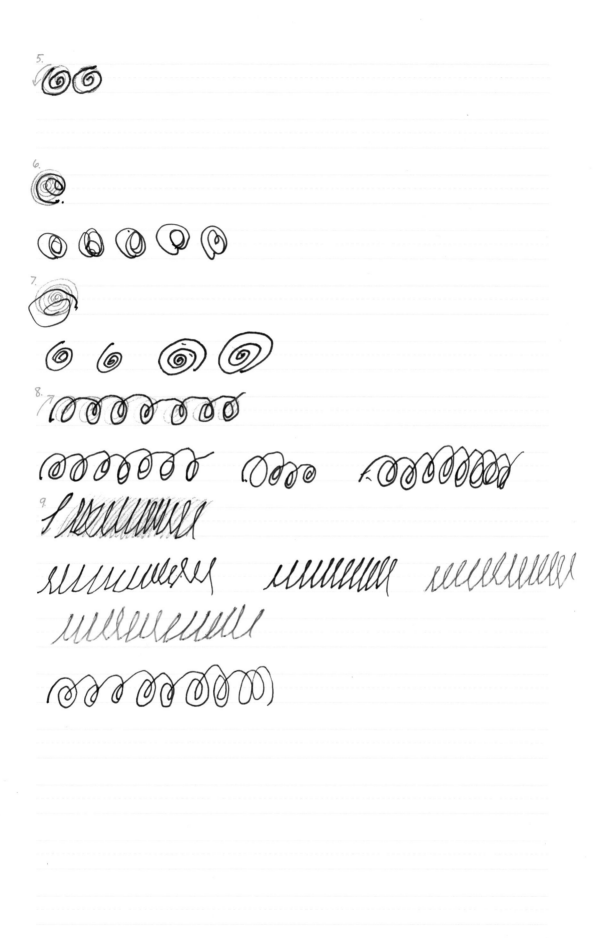

Cursive writing usually has a slant, or slope, to the letters. This angle is not something you need to learn; it is a natural tendency. Faster writing tends to create more of a slope. Everyone has a natural rhythm to their strokes. Getting into your rhythm allows for letter spacing and slope to become effortless and adds to the ease and enjoyment of writing.

TIP: *If you are a lefty, your cursive may have a slope that leans slightly to the left, which is perfectly fine.*

Complete a whole page of each of the following exercises, trying to remain relaxed yet mindful of the forms, until you start to notice your own natural slope and rhythm take over.

three

Print Handwriting

Printed letters are usually easier to read than joined, or cursive, letters. Some people, however, find that joining up letters slows them down and leads to illegible writing. They feel that sticking to separate letters works best for them, and they like the clean, straightforward look of a printed hand.

In this chapter we will look at two styles of printing. Lessons 6 and 7 (see pages 28 to 32) cover the "ball-and-stick" method of printing you may have learned in early grade school. Lessons 9 to 12 (see pages 35 to 44) provide an introduction to printed italic letterforms. These letterforms are the foundation for the cursive handwriting model in chapter 4. Learning how to write the italic alphabet will lay the groundwork for cursive writing of any type.

If your current handwriting seems too angular or pointy to you, going back to these circular shapes may help soften those angles when you incorporate them into your cursive writing. The letterforms look simple, but they take a bit of time due to the number of pen lifts.

TIP: *This no-slant style is great for filling out official forms, where legibility is more important than personality.*

Based on a circle, the letters are formed slowly and carefully. Only four of the lowercase letters are done in one stroke: c, l, o, and s. First trace each letter a few times. Follow the letter's starting point and direction of strokes carefully. Then draw the letters on your own.

aaa bbb ccc

ddd eee fff

ggg hhh iii

jjj kkk lll

mmm nnn ooo

ppp qqq rrr

sss ttt uuu

vvv www xxx

yyy zzz

TIP: *Like most of the lowercase letters, the capitals are also made with several pen lifts, which means they aren't built for speed.*

Sometimes it works best to revisit the original forms you learned, and this is true with writing these capital letters. Whether you are using them with the lowercase letters or on their own as a complete handwriting script, the shapes will be familiar.

EEE   FFF

GGG   HHH

III   JJJ

KKK   LLL

MMM   NNN

OOO   PPP

QQQ   RRR

SSS   TTT

UUU   VVV

WWW   XXX

YYY   ZZZ

"All the world's a stage, and all the
men and women merely players.
They have their exits and their
entrances; And one man in his
time plays many parts."

(Shakespeare As you Like It, *Act 2, Scene 7)*

Now copy this quote, and try to maintain consistency in size, shape, and rhythm.

Lesson 8 Letter patterns for practice

These deceptively simple exercises will train your writing muscles to create the shapes you will use in both printed and cursive italic. The next four lessons (9 to 12, see pages 35 to 44) will introduce the letters in their families of similar shapes, rather than alphabetically. The exercises will help you become accustomed to the letterforms, although while completing the lessons, you should think of them merely as shapes, not as parts of letters.

TIP: *Stick with the specific shapes presented in this exercise until creating them becomes seamless and automatic.*

Do the exercises mindfully, and by the page full. The exercises will help you find your natural slope and rhythm, and with practice, the letterforms will become automatic.

G ooooooooo

S oooooooooooo

W wwwwwwwww

f ffffffffffff

The next four lessons focus on the italic alphabet. By *italic*, we mean letterforms based on the historic style of calligraphy used in Italy during the Renaissance. In this style the letters lean forward, and subsequently the word *italic* has come to mean all typeface letters with a forward slant. The examples are presented in the Getty-Dubay typeface by Barbara Getty and Inga Dubay, teachers who have been internationally recognized as leaders in the field of handwriting improvement. This alphabet is the best style for learning the correct construction of letterforms. As you practice these letters, carefully note where to start each letter, and in which direction to make each stroke. Knowing these positions will help you when you begin to use them in cursive writing.

TIP: *All the "a"-related family letters are single-stroke letters, written with no pen lifts.*

The counter (or body) of the "a" is the most distinctive shape of the italic alphabet. The letters a, d, g, and q use the "a" shape, while the letters b and p feature the same shape upside down. Notice that the shape is a little like a softened triangle, with the top being almost flat along the horizontal.

a d g q b p

a a a   *d d d*

g g g   *q q q*

qda   agd

bbb   ppp

bap   pad

qpd   gda

PRINT AND CURSIVE HANDWRITING WORKBOOK

The italic "n"-related family is also called the branching family of letters, because the hump stroke springs from the baseline and branches out organically from the letter's stem. These letters are n, h, m, and r. An upside-down version of the "n" shape is used for u and y.

n h m r u y

TIP: *Create these letters with a single stroke.*

nnn   hhh

mmm   rrr

mnr   hnr

nhr   uuu

yyy   yum

myn   hun

The "o"-related family consists of o, e, c, and s. These are single-stroke letters. The s fits into the shape of the o. The rest of the alphabet is a mix of single- and double-stroke letters. The straight and narrow family includes the i, j, l, t, and f. For t and f, you'll need two strokes because of the crossbar, and the i and j need a pen lift to make the dot. The diagonals family consists of k, v, w, x, and z.

o e c s i j l t f

k v w x z

o o o   e e e

c c c   s s s

i i i   j j j

l l l   t t t

fff   kkk

vvv   www

xxx   yyy

zzz

"doubt that the stars are fire, doubt that the sun doth move, doubt truth to be a liar, but never doubt I love."

(Shakespeare, Hamlet, Act 2, Scene 2)

Now copy this quote, using your newly learned lowercase letterforms.

TIP: *Focus your practice on one group until you feel comfortable making the letters. Then move on to the next group.*

These capitals are graceful and a good fit to use as a print handwriting for all capitals. They are also the foundation for fancier capitals that can be used to personalize your cursive handwriting. When you look at all the capital letters together, you will notice some are wider or narrower than others. It is best to learn them divided into their various width families, because their width is an essential characteristic of their shapes:

TIP: *Use all capitals for design variation or to emphasize words of particular importance.*

▶ The narrow ones: B, E, F, L, P, R, S, I, and J
▶ The medium ones: H, A, V, N, T, U, X, Y, Z, and K
▶ The wide or round ones: O, Q, C, G, and D
▶ And the extra-wide ones: W and M

B E F L P R
S I J

BBB   EEE

FFF   LLL

PPP   RRR

SSS   III

JJJ

H A V N T U
X Y Z K

HHH   AAA

VVV   NNN

TTT   UUU

XXX   YYY

ZZZ   KKK

O Q C G D

OOO   QQQ

CCC   GGG

DDD

W M

WWW   MMM

"A HEART TO LOVE, AND IN THAT HEART, COURAGE, TO MAKE LOVE KNOWN"

(Shakespeare, Macbeth, *Act 2, Scene 3)*

Now try writing the quote above in capital letters. Write it several times, and include your personal slope that you discovered in the warm-up exercise for natural slope.

Numerals should match the size of lowercase letters when written with a mix of uppercase and lowercase letters. If you are writing in all capitals, match the size of your numerals with the size of your capitals.

TIP: Numerals never join together and actually need a little extra space between them to look right.

0 1 2 3 4 5 6 7 8 9

000   111   222

333   444   555

666   777   888

999

Lesson 14 Spacing and consistency

Print handwriting is a good place to pay attention to the pattern your writing is creating. Use the guidelines to create letters of the same size. You will achieve a pleasing, uniform look when the letters match each other in size, related shapes, slope, and even spacing. With practice you will become familiar with the letterforms, and your natural rhythm will take over. Consistent rhythm and pattern are essential elements of good handwriting. The best way to achieve this is to start out with lesson 5 (see page 24). When you can make these strokes consistently, move on to writing something you know by heart, such as a poem or the lyrics to a favorite song. Choosing to write something you don't have to think about means you can concentrate on your letters and spacing.

TIP: *Since spacing and consistency are so important, take your time with this lesson. Practice with a number of lyrics, or whatever material you know by heart, to get practice with a wide variety of letter combinations.*

four

Cursive Handwriting

Connecting letters increases your speed by combining some strokes and limiting the number of times you lift your pen off the paper. Cursive also allows you to write in a consistent manner for long periods of time without fatigue.

We'll start with lessons and exercises for each type of connection (called joins) and pay attention to situations in which letters do not connect. Our model alphabet for learning the joins is the italic letters you just encountered in lessons 9 through 12 (see pages 35 to 44). These letter-forms offer good practice for each type of join, plus they are clean and simple in structure and can be written quickly without becoming sloppy. Ensure you are comfortable with how each letter is formed: where it starts, and the direction and sequence of each stroke. This foundation is essential.

Lessons 21 and 22 cover Zaner-Bloser cursive, a more traditional style that's still used by many people.

Lesson 15 Warming up for joins

The italic print you learned in lessons 9 to 12 can be connected to make beautiful, modern cursive that won't fall apart when writing quickly. In this lesson, you'll get a refresher on the italic print alphabet, but with a few letter variations that will help you learn to make proper joins for cursive writing.

First, however, we'll start with some simple warm-ups to help your fingers get used to joining strokes. Start out slowly, then write more quickly until you are working at a comfortable speed. Lift your pen or pencil regularly as you go. A whole line of unbroken joins is not necessary—in handwriting you will be lifting your tool every four to five letters anyway.

TIP: *Longer words in particular need a pen lift or two to give you time to think about spelling as you write.*

mm mm mm rr

nnn oo oo oo

s sy sy sy sy

r r r r r

ζ ζ ζ ζ ζ

a b c d e f g h i j k

l m n o p q r s t u v

w x y z

aaa   bbb

ccc   ddd

eee   fff

ggg   hhh

iii   jjj

kkk   lll

mmm   nnn

ooo   ppp

qqq   rrr

sss   ttt

uuu   vvv

www   xxx

yyy   zzz

Very often you will make a diagonal exit stroke to join to a straight stroke, such as when connecting the a to the p when writing the word *ape*. As you leave a letter to connect to the next, make sure your exit stroke is a straight diagonal. Let it reach up to the waistline before you start the next letter. For a join to the letters i, j, p, u, and y, swoop up to the waistline and start your next letter cleanly with a straight downstroke. This join will make the strokes blend, and it will look as though the two strokes are connected about half-way up the letter. (Note: v and w are exceptions, as they form a peak at their joins with the preceding letter rather than a blended join.) Avoid making a flattened join, with the joining stroke following the baseline rather than reaching up in a diagonal to the waist-line. Flattened joins look a little clunky and will interrupt the flow of your writing.

Yep!

Nope!

The joins meld together at midpoint.

ai au ay ci cu cy
mi mu my hi hu hy

ai ai   *au au*

ay ay   ci ci

cu cu   cy cy

mi mi   mu mu

my my   hi hi

hu hu   hy hy

aj ap ej ep
ni np lj lp
av ev nw lw

Blend your upswing exit stroke with the downward stroke of the following letter.

aj aj   ap ap

ej ej   ep ep

ni ni   np np

lj lj   lp lp

av av   ev ev

nw nw   lw lw

For a join to the ascending letters (b, h, k, l, t), make the same joining stroke you just practiced, but change the exit stroke to a vertical at the waistline and very lightly move it up along the paper or in the air to the starting point of the ascending letter. The word *that* includes two such joins.

ab eb ah ch ck
uk il cl at et

ab ab   eb eb   ah ah   ch ch

ck ck   uk uk   il il   cl cl

at at   et et

TIP: *Note that t is not as tall as a full ascender, but it must be taller than the i or e, which it can be confused with.*

Another type of diagonal exit stroke rolls over to form a hump. This exit used for joining to n, m, r, and x. Sometimes y can be in this group if you prefer to start it with a hump rather than a straight downstroke. Just before your diagonal exit stroke reaches the waistline, roll over and start the downstroke of the next letter. This gives the n its two humps and the m its three humps.

an cn en hn

in kn mn dm

im lm mm um

ar cr ir ax ux

an an   cn cn   en en

hn hn   in in   kn kn

mn mn   dm dm   im im

lm lm   mm mm   um um

ar ar   cr cr   ir ir

ax ax   ux ux

The f, o, r, t, v, w, and x letters end with a horizontal stroke along the waistline that reaches out to the next letter. When you are writing with the italic alphabet, they join into every letter but f. The r needs a tiny dip before the following letter to preserve its shape.

fn fu fy

on ou oy

rn ru ry

tn tu ty

vn vu vy

wn wu wy

xn xu xy

fn fn   fu fu   fy fy

on on   ou ou   oy oy

rn rn   ru ru   ry ry

tn tn   tu tu   ty ty

vn vn   vu vu   vy vy

wn wn   wu wu   wy wy

xn xn   xu xu   xy xy

TIP: The word "fortify" provides five opportunities to practice this join. Just for fun, challenge yourself to find words with several tricky joins, and add them to your daily doodles or formal practice.

Because x and t are two-stroke letters, you can join either stroke to the following letter. For both, if you join from the first stroke, a diagonal exit becomes the joining stroke, and you need to go back to cross your t and cross your x to finish the letter. If you join from the second stroke of the t (the crossbar) you are joining from a waistline horizontal. If joining from the second stroke of the x, your join is also a horizontal but very short, and made by drawing this crossbar from the lower left to the upper right and adding on a little horizontal.

tn ti to ty xy
xo xi xn

tn tn   ti ti

to to   ty ty

xy xy   xo xo

xi xi   xn xn

The final stroke of some letters (b, p, and s) ends on the left side of the letter rather than the right. The pen must retrace the last stroke along the baseline to join to the following letter. This horizontal stroke becomes a diagonal as it leaves the letter and follows the rules for joining to a following letter with a diagonal. The lowercase z follows this same pattern. Because these joins require a reversal of the direction of your writing, you may find them slow and more cumbersome to make. Z ends with a horizontal that swings up into a diagonal, following the same joining rules.

The diagonals reach out to the next letter as a rollover join or a straight join.

TIP: *When you write quickly, a loop is often formed by not precisely retracing the bottom stroke. This is fine, as long as the letters remain legible with this variation.*

ba be bk bo bu

bj pa pe pl po

pu sa sl so st

sp sc za zi

zo zu

ba ba   be be

bk bk   bo bo

bu bu   bj bj

pa pa   pe pe

pl pl   po po

pu pu   sa sa

st st   so so

st st   sp sp

sc sc   za za

zi zi   zo zo

zu zu

PRINT AND CURSIVE HANDWRITING WORKBOOK

If a letter you're joining begins on its right side rather than its ts left, the join into this letter is a little tricky. This will happen when you join into the letters a, c, d, g, o, q, and s. You will need to bring the previous exit stroke, whether a diagonal or a horizontal, up to the starting point of each of these following letters. This means your pen will move forward and then back along the same line to form the top of the letter.

Switchback joins are easiest when they follow a horizontal waistline exit, because your pen is already at the top of the letter.

TIP: *Be sure your letters have a flat top and you are not adding a loop; be especially careful not to make c look like an e by adding a loop. Also, you'll need to close the o by starting it far enough to the right (it can look like a u if it is left open).*

ia oa wa ac ad

id ag ig fo mo

oo to iq es is

ns ps us zs

ia ia   oa oa   wa wa

ac ac   ad ad   id id

ag ag   ig ig   fo fo

mo mo   oo oo   to to

iq iq   es es   is is

ns ns   ps ps   us us

zs zs

Some letters are awkward and need extra care when making joins. For example, the italic shapes of r, s, z, b, f, and e are hard to join into or out of. You may wish to incorporate alternate forms for these letters from the Zaner-Bloser model which you will learn in lessons 22 and 23, (see pages 78 to 91). On the next page, practice some of the most common two- and three-letter combinations. Use them to try out your joining skills, and make note of any combinations you might need to change or leave unjoined for legibility or ease of writing.

> **TIP:** Just as you proof material that you type, get in the habit of rereading what you write by hand, particularly if it is written for readers other than yourself, so that you can fix any letters and joins that may be confusing.

bears	brass	fresh
fuzzy	fist	mars
zap	after	freezes
tufts	rise	or
te	the	and

ing   ion   tion

ent   ati   for

her   hat   ere

con   his   all

ons   men   ith

ons   ve   rev

was   com   per

eve

ist   ear   be

om   our

Here are some of the letters and joins that are most often done poorly, leading to illegible words:

▶ Looping i so it is confused with e.
▶ Joining into r, n, and m without the first stroke of these letters. This usually happens for people who start these letters at the bottom rather than the top.
▶ Forgetting to round the arches of the n-related letters, so they become indistinguishable from u.
▶ Drawing the single stroke e too tall, so it becomes confused with i.
▶ Writing t with a loop rather than a single stroke can make it look like an l, or an e if you forget to cross it.
▶ The alternate r written without its "shelf" (sloping downward too soon) becomes confused with the alternate s (the s shaped like a little sailboat).

Practice anything you are still having trouble with in the space below.

The capitals for the italic alphabet can be plain or dressed up. The flourishes here are called *swashes* and are extensions of one or more strokes of the printed letter. Almost any stroke can be lengthened into a swash, but the letters in the exercise are the basic forms. Think of the swashes as a bit of elegance in your writing. When we talk about flourishes in lesson 30 (see page 110), you will see how you can extend a swash to become a full flourish.

When practicing these capitals, do not join them up to the letter following them. Write them at the same slope as your other letters and make sure they have room for the swash in front. Again, a good exercise is to write capitalized words, several on one line.

TIP: *Swashes must never be stiff or awkward. Give them room to breathe. They need to happen away from the stem of the letter, so they never look crowded or squashed.*

A B C D
E F G H
I J K L M
N O P Q
R S T U V
W X Y Z

A A A   B B B

C C C   D D D

E E E   F F F

G G G   H H H

I I I   J J J

K K K   L L L

M M M   N N N

O O O   P P P

Q Q Q   R R R

S S S   T T T

U U U   V V V

W W W   X X X

Y Y Y   Z Z Z

Here are some words to practice swash capitals and lowercase letters as well as your joins.

Armenia   Barbados

Chad   Denmark

Ecuador   Fiji

Greece   Haiti

Ireland   Jamaica

Kuwait   Latvia

Mexico   Nepal

Oman   Peru

Qatar   Rwanda

Slovakia   Togo

Uzbekistan   Venezuela

Wales   Xalapa

Yemen   Zimbabwe

The Zaner-Bloser alphabet was developed in 1888 as the beautiful and distinguished model for cursive handwriting. It is flowing and lovely, and for many decades it was taught in schools as the foundation for good penmanship. Many of you will recognize these letterforms from your original handwriting instruction.

& the cemetery. Your home is beautiful & welcoming, and I will look forward to staying here again. Your back atio is perfect for sitting & reading. You are a lovely

Flowing, beautiful Zaner-Bloser

In addition to providing alternate letterforms for problematic italic letters, this alphabet has lovely ascenders and descenders. If you like the decorative appearance of loops in your writing, now is the perfect time to include some looped letters in your alphabet. The looped forms of ascenders and descenders also make joining to following letters easier. Without a loop, you need to lift your pen after any descender. Lifting is a little faster (loops tend to slow down handwriting), but you might prefer the shape and flow of a loop connecting to the following letter, or a fancy loop to finish off a line of writing.

Zaner-Bloser is best written rather slowly, because it can easily fall apart with speed, becoming sloppy and illegible. Be thoughtful about which forms from this model you choose for quickly written handwriting. Follow the model closely for this lesson. As you practice these letterforms, notice where your hand wants to deviate from the model. Stick with the model for now; there will be time later to start breaking the rules.

a a a　　　b b b

c c c　　　d d d

e e e　　　f f f

g g g　　　h h h

i i i　　　j j j

k k k　　　l l l

m m m　　　n n n

o o o　　　p p p

q q q   r r r

s s s   t t t

u u u   v v v

w w w   x x x

y y y   z z z

TIP: *The t in this alphabet is the only letter with a crossbar. For a more modern variation, make it a bit shorter so it can join out of the crossbar.*

Most joins in this alphabet are very simple, swinging up from the baseline to begin the following letter. Even the descenders loop up to the waistline, so you can easily join out of them.

abc   def

ghi   jkl

mno   pqr

stu   vwx

yz

The letters b, o, v, and w reach out to the following letter with a slightly dipped horizontal. The letters a, c, d, g, o, and q are a little tricky to join into, as they start on their right side, the opposite side from the preceding letter's exit. To join into them, you need to travel up and over to the starting point of these letters, and then back along your stroke as you draw the letters. If you drag a diagonal exit through these letters to get to the starting point, you will add a loop to your letter, which will make it messy and harder to read. Here are joins to practice. Try to do them cleanly, and become comfortable with them. You can always choose not to join into any of the letters that give you too much trouble.

back   *bit*

bunt   *open*

over   *on*

out   *wet*

will   *wand*

vet   *van*

vine   tan

lap   cat

ick   mac

ucd   und

id   nudge

egg   beg

ign   no

too   so

PRINT AND CURSIVE HANDWRITING WORKBOOK

boa   tqu

squ   dqn

iqu

Capitals are special. They are not used very often compared to the lowercase letters, so they can be a visual resting place for the reader, indicate a new thought, or add a point of emphasis by the way you write them. You can write them so they stand out or fit in nicely with the line of writing.

TIP: *Here are two simple hacks to make these letters more graceful:*

1. *Make the top section of B slightly smaller than the bottom section of the B.*

2. *Make the hump of N and first hump of M the same height as the other letters so that these letters don't look smaller than the rest.*

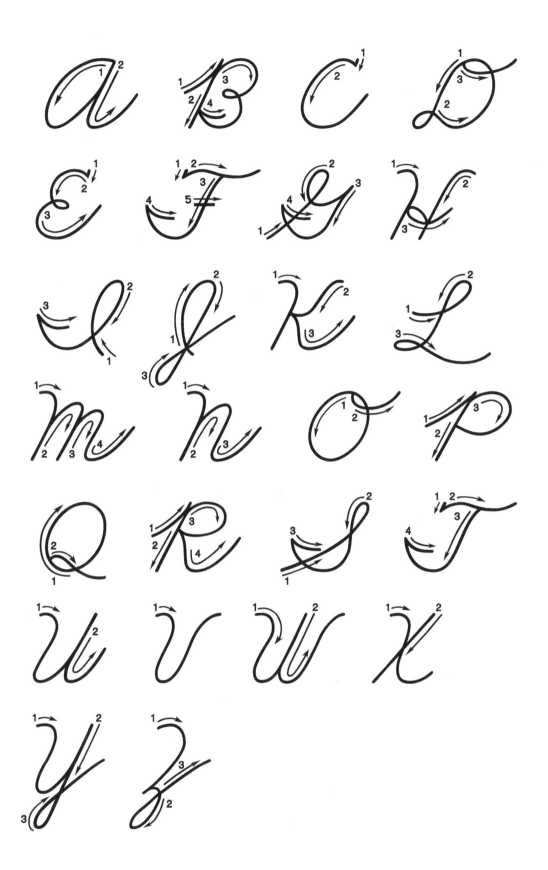

aaa   BBB

CCC   DDD

EEE   FFF

GGG   HHH

III   JJJ

KKK   LLL

mmm   nnn

OOO   PPP

QQQ   RRR

SSS   TTT

UUU   VVV

WWW   XXX

YYY   ZZZ

It is a good idea to practice writing in words rather than single letters whenever possible, because capitals are best learned when paired with lowercase letters.

Albatross   Bat

Caterpillar   Dodo

Emu   Fox

Gecko   Heron

Iguana   Jaguar

Kiwi   Lynx

Mole   Newt

Oyster   Pika

Quetzal   Raccoon

Squid   Tiger

Uakari   Vulture

Wolf   Xenops

Yak   Zebu

Lesson 24 Achieving consistency in your writing

For writing to be consistent, the letters need to match each other in basic shape, size, spacing, and slope. In our model italic alphabet, the letters are based not on a circular o but on an oval o. All the other letters follow o's example and are a similar width. You may be comfortable with a condensed oval shape or one slightly wider than the model. Whichever you prefer, all your letters will need to follow this basic width. The form you choose will also determine the size of the letters. Let the letters match each other in width (except for i, l, m, and w) and height. If you have trouble making the body of the lowercase letters the same height, use guidelines to help train your hand to write them more evenly. With a steady shape and size, the spacing will be easy to control.

TIP: *To achieve the goal of consistency with these new letterforms, write out a long piece of text, such as several verses of a song you know by heart. It will probably take at least a full page of writing for your natural rhythm to emerge. Remember to relax and be patient with yourself.*

The joins we review in this chapter will help keep the spacing consistent. The *counter space* is the name given to the space inside the letter, such as the space inside an n or u. A good rule of thumb is to aim for the space between letters to be about the same as the amount of space contained within the counters of the letters. If your o shape is condensed, your whole line of writing will be spaced together a little more tightly than if you have a rounder o. Everything is related.

Finally, check your slope. Try to write with these letters enough that your natural slope starts to dominate, as it did in the exercises in lesson 5 (see page 24). When you become familiar with the letter shapes and joins, the flow of your natural rhythm and slope will take over, and consistency will not be a problem. Pick a poem or song lyrics to write down, and keep these points in mind as you write.

Italic letterforms are built for speed: the oval o; the straight, clean ascenders; the no-nonsense descenders. With these forms as your base, and with whichever alternate forms you include, the next step is to speed your writing up a little. Don't forget to relax as you write!

TIP: *Lift your pen every four to five letters. Not every letter needs to join to the next. Lifting your pen gives you time to think and regroup before the next string of letters. Especially when writing longer words, lift your pen as needed to keep track of spelling.*

Using a timer, write a sentence carefully, in your best handwriting, and note how long it took to write it and how many words are in the sentence. Next, set your timer for the same amount of time and write the same sentence just a little faster. If you have extra time before the timer goes off, start your sentence again. Now, count how many words you wrote. See if you can write a word or two more in the same amount of time. Keep gradually increasing your speed until you are writing either at an uncomfortable pace or your writing is illegible.

Now, slow back down to the amount of writing that is a little faster than your careful writing but still comfortable and flowing. Aim to write at this pace for your normal handwriting.

five

Stylin'!

You have learned how to make your handwriting legible. It's time to make it distinctive! This chapter provides exercises to help you discover the patterns and traits that make up the natural character of your writing. Letting these traits shine through your handwriting adds depth and artistry to your penmanship as well as "voice" to your message, making it more interesting and memorable. Lesson 27 (see page 102) offers suggestions for updating your signature. (Don't forget to fill out a new signature card at the bank if you make signature changes!)

This chapter also offers tips on taking notes at speed and helps you design formal writing for signing cards and special greetings. This chapter is all about injecting personality into your handwriting, whether strong and clear, friendly, fancy, professional, quiet, or vigorous.

Lesson 26 Finding your personal style

Now that you have perfected the model alphabet, found your personal slope and rhythm, and learned the basic joins, you are ready to revise and shape your writing to match your personality. To reveal individualized characteristics in your handwriting, these exercises will push your writing to the breaking point. From there you can analyze what you like and want to keep, and what you want to avoid. Your style might show through in the particular way you form a letter under pressure, or how you create particular joins, or the slope or size of your writing. Adding speed to a strong writing foundation can be very illuminating.

For this exercise, start with a sentence about seven words long. (A good sentence to try is "The offer still stands if you want it.") Write it slowly and carefully. Underneath it, write the sentence again, a bit more quickly, and then under that more quickly still. Continue speeding up until your writing completely falls apart.

Now look at the sentences you wrote. The first should be clean and legible, but it probably will not have much individual character. The second might be about the same. From there on the writing will likely be larger and wider. You should start to see interesting things happening in the third and fourth sentences. After that, what you have written will possibly be illegible.

TIP: *Remember, the first job of writing is to communicate clearly. Check for legibility with any changes you incorporate.*

Take the line you like the best and mark what it is about the writing, overall, that you like. Next, find individual joins or letter shapes that might be breaking the standard rule but are legible and a bit more interesting. Did your double letters change with speed? How about your crossbars? What happened to the width of the letters and the length of the joining strokes? What happened with the ascenders and descenders? Did they get shorter or taller as your writing got faster? Do you like the look of your writing when it is a little wider than the model or a little tighter? Do you like rounded tops and bottoms or more pointed, zigzagged lines of writing? Pull out your favorite bits and pieces from the exercise and try to incorporate them into your more refined writing. You are now in the driver's seat, and can make whatever decisions suit your personal style.

Wishing you the very
happiest New Year!

What a treat to see you
last Friday. I hope the rest
of your trip went well, and that

in Honolulu, and then
another week on Maui.
We lucked out on a great
air B+B, and got to re-visit

Thank you for the
magazines & especially
for thinking of me.
I will not be bored

In the meantime,
I am so happy and
contented here at home

Italic handwriting variations in everyday use.

Double letters don't have to be the same. They always provide an opportunity to add style to your writing. The word *the* appears so often in English, you might develop it into a small design you can repeat each time it comes up.

Lesson 27 Getting more personal

Here is another exercise to help reveal your personal preferences. For this exercise, on a separate piece of paper, write a pangram (a sentence using all the letters of the alphabet). Here are a few of the shorter pangrams:

The five boxing wizards jump quickly.

Sphinx of black quartz, judge my vow.

The quick brown fox jumps over a lazy dog.

Few black taxis drive up major roads on quiet hazy nights.

Write your chosen pangram several times, each time a little faster, *without lifting your pen*, even between words or to dot i's or cross t's. Remember, this is an exercise, not the form your handwriting should be, so it will be weird. Now, take a look. What do you notice about your writing that you like? Are there joins you find interesting? Pull them out and practice them. Will they only work with certain combinations of letters? If so, which letters? The crossbar can change according to the letter before or after the join. Did you use different joins from the crossbar during your speed writing? If so, choose one or two to develop further.

TIP: *Joins that make a letter-sized loop will be mistaken for another letter, so keep legibility in mind, and don't get too wild.*

Write out the joins and letterforms that you like from this exercise. Analyze them to see what will work and remain legible in your everyday writing. These joins and forms will add personality and style to your writing. Practice them as you did the formal letterforms until they are comfortably incorporated into your writing.

PRINT AND CURSIVE HANDWRITING WORKBOOK

Now that you have developed a new style of handwriting, let's focus on your signature. Signatures were first required by law in 1677 with the British Act of Parliament "An Act for Prevention of Frauds and Perjuries."

You may like your signature just as it is, or you may want to experiment with ways to improve it a bit. Maybe it has always bothered you. In this lesson we will treat your signature as a little logo or artistic design. Here are some examples of creative signatures.

You can have two forms for your signature: one that is mostly legible for important documents, and a speeded-up version you can sign with your fingertip on a payment screen or receipt. We will work with the legible one.

Start by writing out your signature. Write it slowly first, then a few times at a faster rate. Analyze and mark what you like and don't like about the results.

Now let's introduce some basic elements of design that relate to handwriting:

▶ Line (horizontal, vertical, straight, diagonal, curved)

▶ Shape (circles, squares, triangles, ovals, flourishes)

▶ Space (room between letters, words, and lines of writing on a page)

▶ Harmony (how all the elements flow together)

Carefully analyze your signature through the lens of these elements. What do you want to keep, emphasize, leave out, or change? This work is best done with tracing paper and a pencil. Try out several ideas, and have fun! Don't erase any of your experiments so you can look back at ideas if you need to.

Line: Are your letters generally spiky or round? Do any lines in your writing stand out more than others? Do you find you have emphasized diagonals, verticals, or horizontals? If you notice you are giving more weight to horizontals, for instance, write your signature again and see if there is another place you can repeat a horizontal, or change a form to be more horizontal. On the subject of lines, some signatures include underlining the signature, or the curved lines of a flourish. These are ideas you can try.

Shape: Draw a loose outline of your signature on the page. What shape is it? Roundish? Long and thin, tall and rectangular? Do you like it or do you want to change it? Work with the overall shape until you find something you like better. You might even leave out letters if your name remains legible, or you may decide to use just your first initial and keep your last name intact. Next, notice the shapes of the letters. Are they clean and geometric? Are they angular or soft? Find ways to emphasize these traits. Now is a good time to choose your capitals. Play with the forms, enlarge them, add flourishes, anything you like. They will be the focal point of your little design, so try out lots of ideas. For example, you could try enlarging the capital letters to the point that some of your lowercase letters are written inside the capitals' spaces.

Space: Do you prefer words that have their letters close together or more open? Some letters can be stretched wide and remain legible, and others can't. The letter w, for example, keeps its readability whether it is much wider than all the other letters, whereas an o needs to remain closed to not be confused with other letters. If the u is too spiky and doesn't keep its curve at the bottom, it is just a zigzag, and the n has the same problem if the shape of its hump is too pointed. So when you are playing with spacing, keep the basic letterforms as your guide unless changing them does not hurt the legibility too much.

Harmony: There should be a sense of unity among all the elements of your signature. You want your signature to flow smoothly from your pen and look freely written rather than labored over. Practice your new design over and over until it becomes an easy expression of who you are.

Lesson 29 Taking notes

Advances in neuroscience regarding note-taking and information retention indicate that students who take notes by hand retain more information than those who type their notes. A new phenomenon called "the drawing effect" was observed in a 2016 study by Jeffrey D. Wammes and his team of researchers. This study showed that including diagrams, drawings, 1 or even just doodles in your notes helps you retain the information better. So free up your page for unorthodox note-taking and doodle away!

Here are a few tips for getting your ideas down quickly during a lecture or presentation:

▶ Divide your paper into smaller areas. Writing long lines of text across your notebook is not necessary and can slow you down. A narrower writing area will remind you to capture the gist of an idea. See the Cornell note-taking system in the illustration on this page.

▶ Do more listening than writing, and jot down only the important points. Verbatim notes are not necessary.

▶ Do not write in full sentences. Some people find that leaving out the verbs speeds up their note-taking, and verbs are easy to remember when fleshing out the notes later.

▶ Use boxes, lines, colors, or bolder writing to highlight essential information or direct quotes.

Cornell note-taking system of paper division

Practice these skills using a notebook to take notes on a podcast, an online lecture, or a TED talk.

Lesson 30 Put a bow on it

When you write for others, you want your handwriting to be readable. More than that, there are times when you want a message to look special. It's a good idea to prepare for such times, and it's easy (and fun!). In this lesson you will develop a pattern for your message that you can have at the ready. You won't have to labor over how to make your writing match the moment. Like preparing for a performance by practicing a piece of music, the work you do in this lesson will ensure you have a solid design available for any occasion.

Start with several thumbnail sketches. A thumbnail sketch is a quick, abbreviated drawing of an idea. Usually such a note will only be a few lines of writing, like "Have a Happy Birthday!" or "We miss you, get well soon!" Use horizontal lines for the writing (keep these short, representing one or two words per line), and use scribbles for other elements like capitals or flourishes. Your own signature will be the final touch in each design. Play with several ideas, varying the size of the words and the overall shape of the design. You can refer back to the design elements you worked with during your signature development in lesson 28 (see page 106). Next, choose one or two thumbnail designs to develop into your message pattern.

Thumbnail sketches for designing a short message

To add a flourish, follow a few simple rules. Just as with the swashes for capitals, a flourish should not crowd the letter but should grow out from a stroke of the letter in an organic manner. Flourishes need to be fluid and free. One basic underlying structure of a flourish is the figure eight, where the line moves to the right, turns around in a graceful loop, and curves over to the left and back again loosely following a sideways "8" shape. This shape can be varied by rounding it more to get more height, widening it to make it more horizontal, or adding or subtracting loops. See the bonus lesson 5 in the next chapter for more help with flourishes (see page 130).

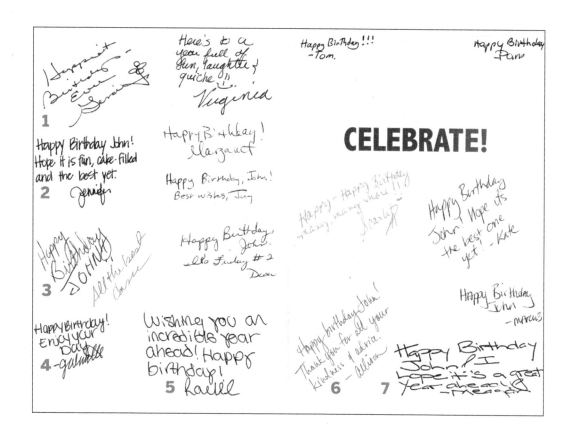

1. Playful entrance and exit strokes are echoed in the capital G and E. Her letter joins are elongated, and the x-height is very small, giving her message a light feel. The floral illustration with her signature adds charm.

2. This message demonstrates strength and style. The letters do not join but are upright and close together. The shapes of the signature's capital J and ending r mirror each other nicely.

3. & 4. Emphasizing important words ("John" and "Enjoy your day") through size and letterform adds visual interest to these messages.

5. This message is clear and full of personality. The y in "Birthday" starts from the upper right, loops at the bottom, and exits at the upper left, an easy movement for a leftie. The backward slant of the letters adds character.

6. This beautifully flowing handwriting conveys joy and warmth.

7. The size and letter shapes, which are based on a horizontal oval (note the o in "John" and the two p's in "Happy") help this message stand out. The letters are consistent in width, creating rhythm. Even the horizontal strokes (note the capital H and I are elongated).

In pencil, try out several of your own thumbnail sketches for card signing here.

Calligraphy, a Touch of Elegance

Calligraphy—"beautiful writing," from the Greek words kalli for beauty and graphos for writing—is a perfect way to add a touch of elegance to a special communication, such as an invitation. The last several decades have seen a worldwide resurgence in the art and study of calligraphy. Calligraphers are using social media to share their work and inspire each other. New access to artists in a variety of cultures and native writing systems is resulting in an explosion of creativity in this art form, as well as engendering new collaborations. Calligraphy guilds, workshops, and regional and international conferences are welcoming new artists and ideas. It is a good time to jump into calligraphy!

Italic calligraphy has four distinct features:

▶ It uses a diagonal pen angle.

▶ Each letter leans forward, giving the hand a flowing appearance.

▶ The shape of the letter a and its family group are very important.

▶ The letters and words are placed rather closely together.

For calligraphic handwriting, you will want a fountain pen with a "calligraphy" (also called "blunt or "italic") tip rather than a "round" tip. If you write small, you will want a fine or extra fine tip. If you write large, buy a nib with a bigger tip.

Start your calligraphy practice with a calligraphy marker. Most come with a 3.5 mm chisel edge (a pen tip with a broad edge rather than a pointed tip) on one end and a 2 mm chisel edge on the other. (Try the Zig® or the Tombow® calligraphy markers.) The wider marker edge makes it easier to feel how your tip is touching the paper, and to see if the tip is making a solid line on the paper. Hold your marker edge at a 45° pen angle.

The most fundamental aspect of writing with a chisel edge pen is holding a consistent pen angle. The pen angle refers to the alignment of the chisel edge tip with the baseline. The edge can be completely in line with the baseline ("flat" pen angle) or the edge's right corner can be twisted as much as 45° ("diagonal" pen angle). The pen angle controls the width of each stroke and creates the curved strokes' alternating thinning and thickening swell.

TIP: *Lefties! You might want to pass on the markers and go straight to a dip pen, which has a metal nib that you dip into ink. You can buy nibs that are cut at a slant just for lefties. This slant makes holding the pen angle for calligraphy much easier for you.*

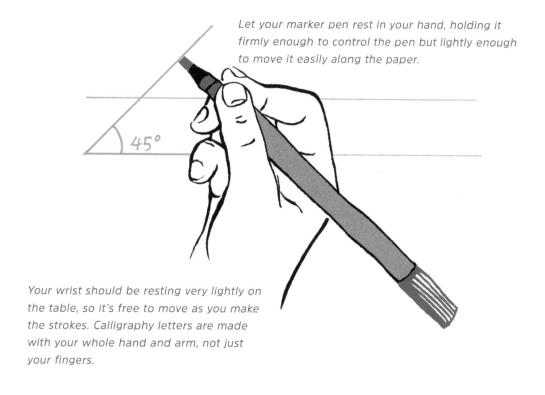

Let your marker pen rest in your hand, holding it firmly enough to control the pen but lightly enough to move it easily along the paper.

45°

Your wrist should be resting very lightly on the table, so it's free to move as you make the strokes. Calligraphy letters are made with your whole hand and arm, not just your fingers.

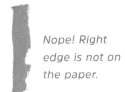 *Nope! Right edge is not on the paper.*

 Nope! Left edge is not on the paper.

 Yep! Even pressure is on both edges.

The tip of your calligraphy marker has two corners you need to be aware of. Make sure both corners of your marker tip are always on the paper for the entire stroke, especially on the curves. This is the first step: keeping track of your all-important pen angle throughout each stroke.

Here are some strokes to try out to see how the 45° pen angle affects each shape.

Notice how the thickness of the line changes.

Downstrokes are thicker than horizontal strokes.

Upstrokes along the diagonal are the thinnest strokes.

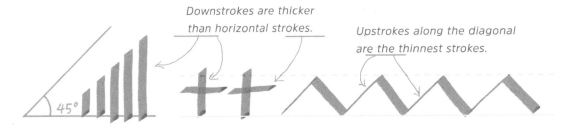

Remember to hold both edges of your calligraphy marker tip on the paper, and move slowly and carefully.

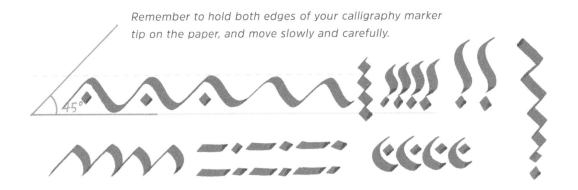

Try out the strokes you've learned on the following practice page. When you feel you have mastered control of the pen angle, switch to your fountain pen and work with the letter shapes from lesson 8 (see page 33).

Try out everything you've learned here on the practice lines.

Guidelines for the height and slope of calligraphy letters are based on the size of the pen's edge. If you are using a 2 mm pen edge, the standard italic size of five pen nibs high for the counters means the letters a, c, e, i, and so on will be 10 mm high. For this reason, a smaller nib will be best for handwriting. You can write smaller letters with a larger nib, but your letters will look much heavier than standard italic. Here are basic guidelines and how the letters fit on them:

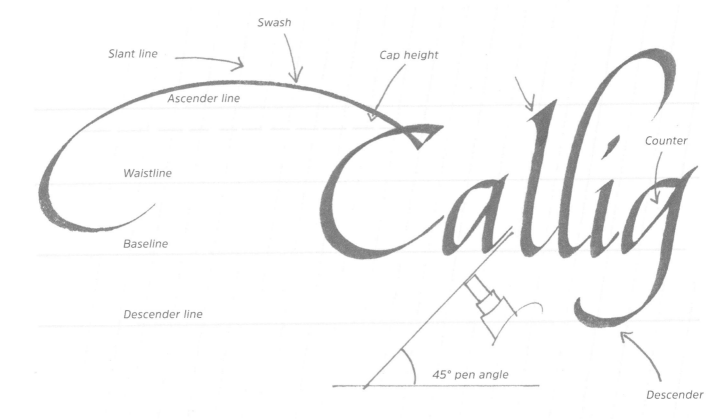

TIP: *The best slope for italic calligraphy is one that leans forward about 10° rather than backward. This is because the pen angle relates in a specific way to the slope as well as the baseline. However, for calligraphic handwriting, go ahead and use your natural slope if that is most comfortable for you.*

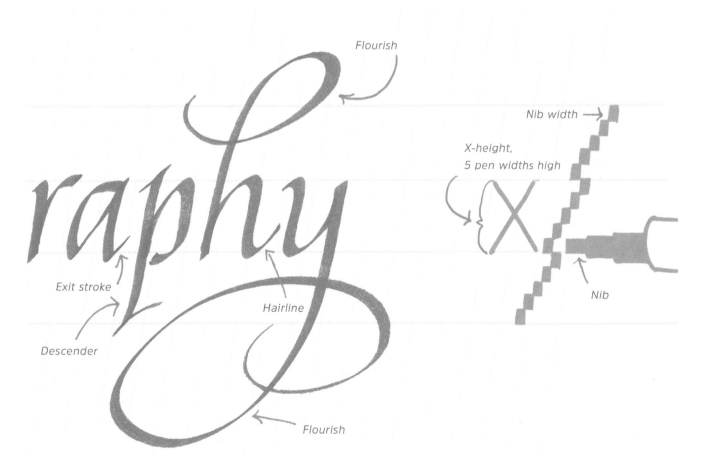

Flourish

Nib width →

X-height,
5 pen widths high

Nib

Exit stroke

Hairline

Descender

Flourish

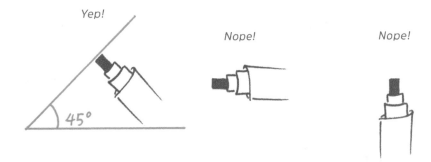

Yep!

45°

Nope!

Nope!

As you have learned, letters are all built from a small number of common shapes. Each stroke is a building block, and each letter is made up of different blocks.

With your fountain pen, try out these basic letter strokes using your own natural slope.

Downstroke: *A stroke made by moving the pen or brush downward on the paper; this stroke is usually thick.*

Upstroke: *A stroke made by moving the pen or brush upward on the paper; this stroke is usually thin.*

Overturn: *A type of stroke (starting or within a letter) where the line changes from thin to thick as it turns.*

Underturn: *A type of stroke (finishing or within a letter) where the line changes from thick to thin as it turns.*

Crossbar: *A thin horizontal stroke used in letters like "t" and "A."*

A little thinner

A little thicker

Compound curve: *A stroke joining the exit from one letter to the entrance of the next; a compound curve can also be a form within a letter.*

As you have learned from the introduction to italic letterforms in chapter 3 (lessons 9 to 12, see pages 35 to 44), the italic letters relate to one another by shape and belong to various "families" that use the same basic strokes. The "a" family is very important to the formation of a refined italic hand. Review their basic forms shown in lessons 9 and 12 (see pages 35 and 41), then note how they appear written with the calligraphy nib in the italic example.

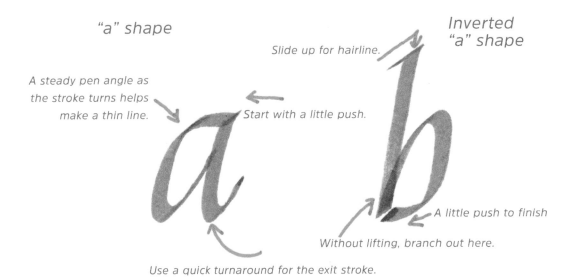

"a" shape

Inverted "a" shape

Slide up for hairline.

A steady pen angle as the stroke turns helps make a thin line.

Start with a little push.

A little push to finish

Without lifting, branch out here.

Use a quick turnaround for the exit stroke.

TIP: *Spend most of your time perfecting the a. It is the most distinctive feature of the italic alphabet, and the most beautiful.*

Bonus Lesson 4
The remaining lowercase italic letters

In chapter 3, you learned the basic shapes, strokes, and families that the remaining lowercase italic letters belong to. Please review their important strokes and the sequences of strokes in lessons 10 and 11 (see pages 37 to 40).

Using the italic example page here, try the letters out first with your larger 3.5 mm marker before writing smaller with your 2 mm tip or your fountain pen.

On these exercise pages, pay close attention to flow and consistency, and watch your pen angle! Write out a paragraph of anything you know by heart. Write the same paragraph several times before dropping down in size and writing it with your fountain pen. The joins follow the same rules as in chapter 4 (lessons 14 to 19, see pages 46 to 68).

TIP: *Remember, not every letter needs to connect to another. Lift your pen and give yourself time to collect your thoughts before tackling a difficult letter or word. If you are writing with consistent letterforms, your calligraphic handwriting will look connected.*

NEED TO KNOW:

*Pen angle 45°, diagonal
X-height five pen nibs,
Slope 10°*

Ascender line

Waistline

Baseline

*Descender/
ascender line*

Italic

*Numbers can all be the same X-height, or
3, 5, 7, and 9 can descend two pen nibs below the baseline,
and 6 and 8 can ascend two pen nibs above the waistline.*

Capitals can take a starring role in handwriting. They can break up the monotony of a line of writing by taking up more space. They can start out a paragraph with a big splashy flourish, or they can be the main element in a designed message (such as the one you crafted in lesson 30 [see page 110]). Not every capital needs to stand out, but it is good to become comfortable with capitals and to use them as a visual pause within your writing.

Following are the italic swash capitals you have seen before. When written with the chisel edge nib, they are agile and distinctive.

Practice these capitals slowly. They do not connect to each other or to the lower-case letters. Give them plenty of room. No matter how flowing it is, if a letter is crowded, it will lose its gracefulness. The best way to work with capitals is to write them in lines of capitalized names, countries, towns, etc. This way you can see how much space they demand.

Finally, we will study the calligraphic flourish. This example page sets out the most basic forms of the flourishes and the ways they grow out of a letter. Plan carefully for the shape, size, and placement of each flourish. This can be done very lightly in pencil, or with tracing paper placed over the line or word to be flourished.

Italic Swash Capitals

Slope 10°
Cap line
3.5 mm
45° pen angle
Baseline

This hump must be to the left of the main stem.

These italic capitals go well with your lowercase italic. The large swashes make them a little bit fancy, but not too much. Make sure the swashes happen away from the body of the letter.

PRINT AND CURSIVE HANDWRITING WORKBOOK

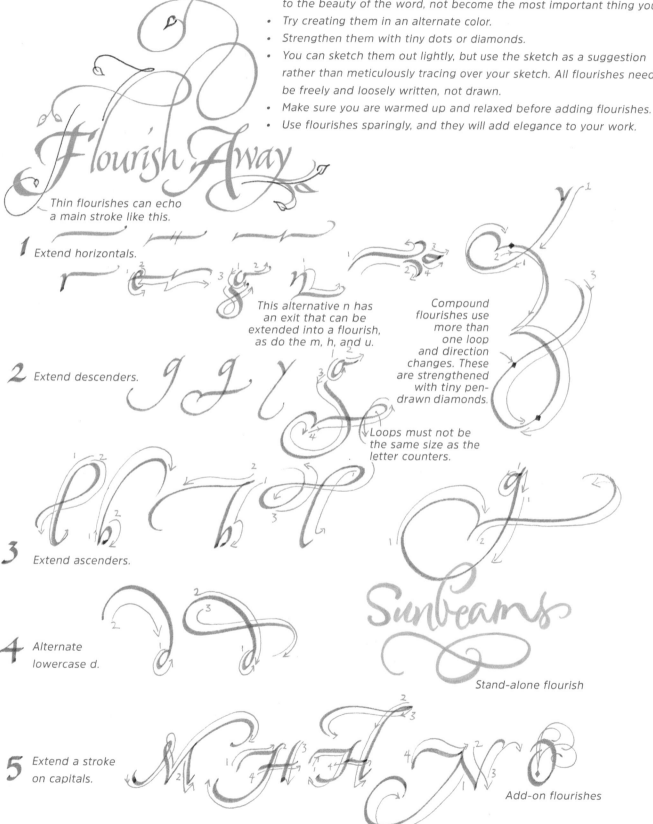

A few tips on flourishes:

- They need room! Don't try and fit them in between lines of writing, or in small spaces. Think of them as graceful dancers that need to avoid banging into a ceiling or wall.
- Memorize a few favorites and use them conservatively. They should add to the beauty of the word, not become the most important thing you see.
- Try creating them in an alternate color.
- Strengthen them with tiny dots or diamonds.
- You can sketch them out lightly, but use the sketch as a suggestion rather than meticulously tracing over your sketch. All flourishes need to be freely and loosely written, not drawn.
- Make sure you are warmed up and relaxed before adding flourishes.
- Use flourishes sparingly, and they will add elegance to your work.

Thin flourishes can echo a main stroke like this.

1 Extend horizontals.

This alternative n has an exit that can be extended into a flourish, as do the m, h, and u.

Compound flourishes use more than one loop and direction changes. These are strengthened with tiny pen-drawn diamonds.

2 Extend descenders.

Loops must not be the same size as the letter counters.

3 Extend ascenders.

4 Alternate lowercase d.

Stand-alone flourish

5 Extend a stroke on capitals.

Add-on flourishes

Conclusion

You have a lot to be proud of! Handwriting is a matter of habit, and habits are hard to change. You have rigorously analyzed your handwriting. You have chosen which parts of your handwriting to keep and what to throw out. You have used simple changes, like paper tilt or relaxing exercises to improve your writing, and you have developed further improvements with long sessions of more intense practice. Beyond that, you will nail that office card signing because you have designed a little pattern for your short messages to guide you. Hopefully, your writing has progressed into a style that suits you and your needs and that you feel is a good representation of who you are.

I would like to leave you with this one last thought: It's important that you practice writing frequently, both for your own pleasure and to keep this uniquely personal form of communication alive.

References

Devine, Beth. "Bad Writing, Wrong Medication." Agency for Healthcare Research and Quality 2010. Accessed April 20, 2019. https://www.ahrq.gov/.

Mueller, Pam A., and Daniel M. Oppenheimer. "The Pen Is Mightier than the Keyboard: Advantages of Longhand Over Laptop Note Taking." *Psychological Science (2014).* doi: 10.1177/0956797614524581.

Wammes, Jeffrey D., Melissa E. Meade, and Myra A. Fernandes. "The Drawing Effect: Evidence for Reliable and Robust Memory Benefits in Free Recall." *The Quarterly Journal of Experimental Psychology* 69, no. 9 (2016): 1752–1776. doi: 10.1080/17470218.2015.1094494.

Acknowledgments

Print and Cursive Writing Handbook is the book I need to keep my own handwriting in line. From the days I sat mesmerized by my first grade teacher's long black habit swaying gracefully at the blackboard as she wrote beautiful cursive letters, I was in love with writing. I am grateful to her, and to the many calligraphers who work diligently to keep the art of handwriting alive and who have taken the scribbled word to new heights in their experimental works. I am also grateful to my many students over the years. They continue to surprise me with a new take on something, or a tiny glimpse into their inner selves through their letters. And finally, thanks to all those who write letters, especially to my mother, grandmothers, and the generations before me whose letters still embody their lives and souls.

About the Author

Sally Sanders is a professional artist and calligrapher with more than 40 years of experience working for individual customers and large and small companies. She lives in the western United States, surrounded by mountains, towering sandstone, and wide-open desert. This beauty finds its way into her painting, calligraphy, and writing.

Sally has taught children and adults for more than 35 years and is continually inspired by her students. She believes in the power of written communication, both for the writer and the reader. Helping her students understand and express their thoughts and ideas, whether in art, calligraphy, or handwriting, is an essential component of her teaching.

Most important to Sally is her family, ranging in age from 1 to 93. "From them, I learn love, which is both the object of my creative fire and its source."

CPSIA information can be obtained
at www.ICGtesting.com
Printed in the USA
LVHW081743250320
650984LV00002B/2